What on Earth? Lightning

What on Earth?

Thunder crack crash! Lightning!

You are inside your house during a thunderstorm. What should you not do?

Turn this page to find out!

First published in 2005 by
Book House an imprint of
The Salariya Book Company
25 Marlborough Place
Brighton
BN1 1UB

Please visit The Salariya Book Company at: **www.salariya.com**

HB ISBN 1-905087-27-6
PB ISBN 1-905087-28-4

Visit our website at **www.book-house.co.uk**
for free electronic versions of:
You Wouldn't Want to be an Egyptian Mummy!
You Wouldn't Want to be a Roman Gladiator!
Avoid joining Shackleton's Polar Expedition!
You Wouldn't Want to sail on a 19th-century Whaling Ship!

Due to the changing nature of internet links, The Salariya Book Company has
developed an online list of websites related to the subject of this book.
This site is updated regularly. Please use this link to access the list:
http://www.book-house.co.uk/WOE/lightning

A catalogue record for this book is
available from the British Library.

Printed and bound in China.

Editors: Ronald Coleman
                                      Sophie Izod
Senior Art Editor: Carolyn Franklin
DTP Designer: Mark Williams

What on Earth? Don't open the door

Some people open doors
to let the lightning out.
This is not a good idea –
lightning can strike the
inside of a house
through the open
doorway!

What on Earth? Lightning

Brian Williams

How often does lightning hit the Earth?

Turn to page 15 to find out!

BOOK HOUSE

Contents

What on Earth?

How much **energy** is in a thunderstorm?

A typical thunderstorm has more energy than ten small nuclear bombs!

shocking energy!

Introduction

A bolt of lightning in a dark stormy sky is one of the most spectacular sights in nature. A lightning flash is a gigantic **electrical spark** that leaps from a thundercloud and crackles across the sky. It is the most visible form of electricity. Lightning occurs when some of the electrical energy inside a thundercloud **bursts** free in a blinding flash of light.

So are clouds electric?

No, clouds are made of rain, hail or snow. Fierce winds blow inside a stormcloud causing water droplets and ice crystals to **crash** violently together. This creates static electricity which builds up inside the cloud.

Is electricity everywhere?

Yes. Everything in the Universe is made of atoms which contain tiny charged particles that can create **tingles** of static electricity. You can feel this sometimes when you touch a metal handrail, or if you rub a balloon and put it near your hair. Our word electricity comes from the Ancient Greek word 'elektron'.

What makes lightning?

Inside a thundercloud there are two kinds of **electrical energy**. Positive (+) electrical charges are lighter, so they rise to the top and negative (-) electrical charges are heavier, so they sink to the bottom. When a positive (+) charge and a negative (-) charge 'jump' together we see lightning.

How much power?

A flash of lightning can contain about 1 billion volts of electricity, and could power a 100 watt light-bulb for 3 months!

Positively charged

Positive (+) electrical charges whirl around near the top of a thundercloud, where it is coldest.

Negatively charged

Negative (-) electrical charges build up near the bottom of the cloud.

Positively electrical!

A flash of lightning called a 'leader' comes down from the cloud and attracts a positive charge from the ground called a 'streamer' which leaps up to meet it.

'Leader' comes down

Positively charged Earth

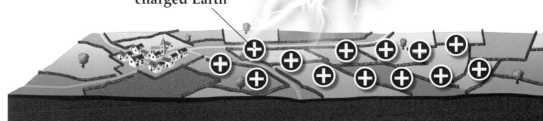

Where does lightning happen?

Thunder and lightning happen during storms. These are caused by hot air rising and cold air rushing in to fill the space. As the ice at the top of a cloud is bumped about it creates an electrical charge and you get lightning. Most areas on Earth have storms.

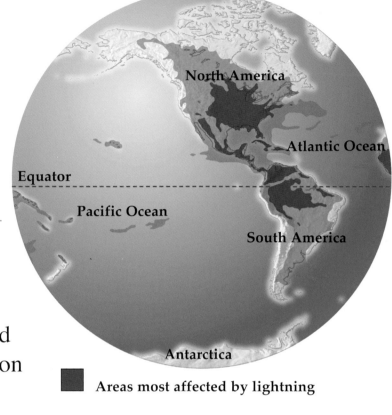

North America

Atlantic Ocean

Equator

Pacific Ocean

South America

Antarctica

■ Areas most affected by lightning

■ Areas less affected by lightning

Baked Alaska?

In June 2004, 17,000 lightning strikes hit Alaska starting hundreds of fires. By the end of June an area twice the size of London was destroyed.

Where are the most thunderstorms?

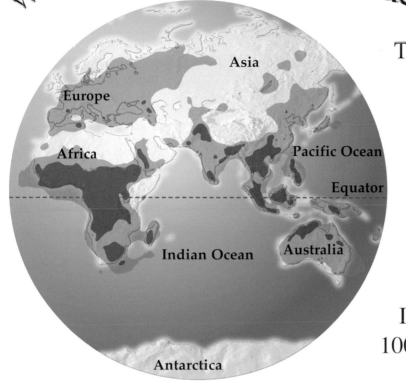

Asia

Europe

Africa

Pacific Ocean

Equator

Indian Ocean

Australia

Antarctica

Thunderstorms are most common near the equator. This is because it's hotter, so there is more hot air to rise and create more thunderclouds and lightning. Areas closest to the equator such as South America, Central Africa and Indonesia have an average of 100-200 thunderstorms a year.

Lightning in space?

Flashes of lightning have been seen on Venus and Jupiter. Lightning on Jupiter is thought to be more powerful than on Earth but happens less often.

Is lightning dangerous?

Lightning is electricity. An electric shock from faulty wiring at home can kill, but the electricity in a lightning flash is much stronger. Fortunately lightning rarely strikes people, but around 100 people in the USA are killed by lightning each year. Lightning can kill people by causing heart failure, or by burning them very badly.

What should you do in a thunderstorm?

There are simple rules for safety. Don't stay outside, and stay away from trees. Never hold metal objects like umbrellas because metal objects attract lightning.

Why should you never shelter under a tree?

During a thunderstorm never shelter under a lone tree or on top of a hill. Lightning usually strikes the highest point as it seeks the shortest route to Earth.

Hotter than the sun?

Lightning makes the air inside a cloud almost 6 times hotter than the surface of the sun!

Lightning, sign of the gods?

Lightning is awesome, so it's not surprising that many years ago people believed it was created by the gods. The ancient Greeks thought lightning was a sign of the gods' anger. They regarded places hit by lightning as sacred and built temples there. The Vikings of northern Europe believed the god Thor caused thunder and lightning by throwing his hammer.

Why did Zeus have thunderbolts?

The Greeks believed that Zeus, king of the gods, showed his anger by hurling thunderbolts down to earth to remind humans that he was all-powerful.

Protection from the God of thunder!

Vikings wore lucky charms for protection. The wearer believed that Thor would not hurl lightning at them!

Yule log!

People thought wood from a 'lightning-blasted' tree would protect them. In Europe, the Christmas 'Yule log' is burned for luck, as well as protection from lightning.

Nettles to protect against a storm?

Vikings prayed to the gods for protection from storms. People hung up nettles, acorns or rosemary to help protect against thunder and lightning.

Is lightning always forked?

Forked or zig-zag are the most common forms, but there are many different kinds of lightning. Sheet lightning is a flash from one thundercloud to another. Ball lightning is a small ball of light which can fly or **hover** inside buildings and planes! Some aircraft pilots have seen 'sprites' or 'rocket lightning' – long streaks of lightning that shoot up in the sky from a cloud, but these are very rare.

How many types of lightning are there?

Forked lightning looks like the letter Y upside down.

Zig-zag lightning is a giant spark that zig-zags its way to the ground.

Sheet lightning makes a white light that fills a wide area of the sky.

Ball lightning is a slow moving ball of fire that can sometimes appear inside structures.

St Elmo's Fire is a faint flickering glow around trees, buildings or ships' masts.

What on Earth?

News flash

Lightning is very common. Around 100 flashes of lightning happen around the Earth every second, but only a quarter of these hit the ground. Most lightning leaps from one cloud to another.

What is a thunderclap?

The hot air inside a thundercloud expands and vibrates and this makes the loud rumbling crash that we call thunder. Thunder and lightning happen at the same time but there's always a gap between the flash of light and the crash of a thunderclap. This is because light travels many times faster than sound.

Flash...BANG!

Count the seconds from the flash of lightning to the bang of thunder. Divide this by 3 and you'll know how many kilometres away the storm is.

Raining cats and dogs?

NO, fish and frogs!

People have found all sorts of weird objects falling from the clouds, including live fish and tiny frogs! These were sucked up from ponds by whirling winds into a storm cloud – and then fell back down with the rain.

Does lightning really never strike twice?

It is said that 'lightning **never strikes** twice', but in fact it can hit the same place many times. Tall skyscrapers are hit by lightning many times each year.

Unlucky elephants!

Elephants aren't always lucky. In 1999, seven elephants in Kruger National Park, South Africa, were killed by the same lightning strike.

What on Earth?

Seven times unlucky!

American park ranger Roy Sullivan has been struck seven times! His injuries include burnt eyebrows, scorched hair and stomach burns. But he's lucky to be alive!

Can planes fly through lightning?

Small planes can be damaged inside a storm cloud. Fortunately, larger aircraft flying through electrical storms are rarely hit by lightning. If lightning does strike, it usually spreads harmlessly over the plane's metal body. However in 1963 in Maryland, USA, a jet airliner was struck, killing 81 people on board. It is the highest **death toll** caused by a single lightning strike.

Could a plane be smashed in a thundercloud?

Yes, howling winds inside a thundercloud whirl around so fast, that they could break up a small plane.

Blob lightning!

In 1984, Russian airline passengers were surprised to see a blob of ball lightning floating over their heads inside the plane! No-one was hurt but the plane's radar was affected.

What on Earth?

Your flight is delayed!

In 1969, the US Apollo 12 spacecraft was hit by lightning as it took off for the Moon. It survived. But in 1987, a rocket launched from Florida crashed after lightning damaged its on-board computer. US shuttle launches are now postponed when lightning is around.

Lightning conductor

21

Is lightning useful?

Scientists can not yet 'harness' the power of lightning, to create electricity. But lightning does enrich the Earth's soil. A lightning flash causes nitrogen and oxygen in the air to bind together. The **nitrogen-rich** raindrops that fall to the ground help fertilise the soil. All plants and animals need nitrogen, and in this way lightning may have helped to create life on Earth.

Fire from the sky!

Prehistoric people probably first discovered fire after lightning struck and set fire to tree branches during a storm.

What on Earth?

shock horror!

In Mary Shelley's story of 'Frankenstein', Dr. Frankenstein uses lightning to bring his monster to life!

What is a lightning conductor?

High buildings and public places are often protected by lightning conductors. A spiked metal rod is fixed to the highest point of a building. A copper strip runs down from the top to wires buried in the ground below. Then if lightning strikes, it travels down the metal conductor leaving the building unharmed.

Do tall towers get struck?

Lightning usually strikes the highest point, so tall buildings are an easy target. The Empire State Building in New York is hit by lightning about 100 times each year. But it is protected by a lightning conductor, so there's no damage. It even protects smaller buildings around it by being a safe conductor for the whole area.

CN Tower
Toronto,
Canada

Sears Tower
Chicago, USA

Eiffel Tower
Paris, France

Empire State
Building
New York,
USA

Petronas Towers
Kuala Lumpur,
Malaysia

What on Earth?

melting rocks!

Lightning generates enormous heat. When a bolt of lightning hits the ground, it is so hot that it can melt solid rock!

Who invented the lightning conductor?

The American scientist Benjamin Franklin (below) proved that lightning was electricity. He invented the lightning conductor in 1752. The first lightning conductor was put on a house in the same year.

The new idea travels!

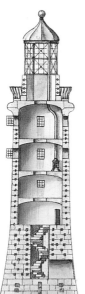

Eddystone Rock Lighthouse near Plymouth was built in 1759 to replace an old wooden lighthouse destroyed by lightning in 1750. It was the first building in Britain to have a lightning conductor.

How fast does lightning travel?

When lightning flashes, it finds the fastest path down to Earth and then it follows the same route back up to the cloud again. A downward flash of lightning (the leader) travels at up to 1,600 kilometres (994 miles) per second. The return or upward speed is even faster at up to 140,000 kilometres (86,990 miles) per second!

Thunder travels much more slowly. A thunderclap moves at the speed of sound, about 350 metres (1148 feet) per second.

How would you survive in a lightning storm?

Some people have been struck by a small flash of lightning and not even noticed it, while others were thrown into the air and had their clothes burnt off their bodies. Follow these simple steps to avoid being hit by lightning.

Lightning Dangers

Telephones Lightning can pass through the wiring and can kill the person speaking.

Open spaces Lightning tries to find the quickest route to Earth, if you are the tallest thing around it may use you! Find shelter immediately.

Swimming Water conducts electricity, which means swimming is very dangerous during storms. Leave the water as soon as possible.

What to do Check-list

Make sure you are inside a **building** as the walls will channel the lightning to the Earth. Use a **radio** to keep track of storms. Use the **Flash to Bang** method (see page 17) to find out how close you are to the lightning. If you can't get inside, make yourself a small target, crouch down with only your feet touching the ground and cover your head.

Lightning facts

In 1977, an aircraft flew into a thunderstorm and all four engines stopped. Lightning struck and the propellers started turning again.

People fishing are twice as likely to be hit by lightning as golfers, both are at risk because they are holding metal.

The Eiffel Tower in Paris is hit by lightning up to 30 times a year.

At any one moment, 2,000 thunderstorms are likely to be happening around the Earth.

There's an area of Florida that is struck by lightning so often, people call it 'Lightning Alley'.

American saguaro cacti are very tall and are often struck by lightning. The water inside the cactus boils off as steam in a split-second, and the cactus explodes!

If there's less than 30 seconds between the flash and the bang, seek shelter. Stay inside for 30 minutes after the last thunderclap. This is called the 30/30 rule.

Glossary

Atom Smallest part of an element (matter), made up of a nucleus, protons and electrons.

Conductor Material which allows heat and electricity to pass through it safely.

Copper Metal that conducts electricity easily.

Electricity Energy in the form of moving electrons.

Equator Imaginary line around Earth's widest part.

Insulation Material that blocks the passage of heat or electricity.

Leader The part of lightning that comes down out of a cloud.

Nitrogen Colourless gas that makes up 80% of the atmosphere (our air).

Particle Very tiny piece of matter, smaller than an atom.

Static electricity Charge of electricity that does not flow as a current along a wire.

Streamer The part of lightning that shoots up from an object in the ground.

Superstitions Beliefs based on folklore and myth.

Volt A measurement of electrical power.

Watt A measurement of electrical power.

What do you know about lightning?

1　What makes thunder?

2　Should you shelter under a tree during a thunderstorm?

3　Who was the Norse god of thunder and lightning?

4　Where are thunderstorms most common?

5　Which lightning is most common?

6　Which travels fastest, thunder or lightning?

7　Who survived the most lightning strikes?

8　Can lightning affect space rockets?

9　Whose monster was brought to life by lightning?

10　Who made the first lightning conductor?

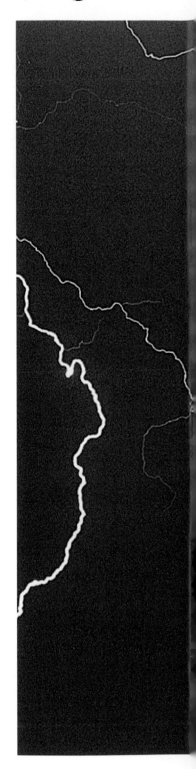

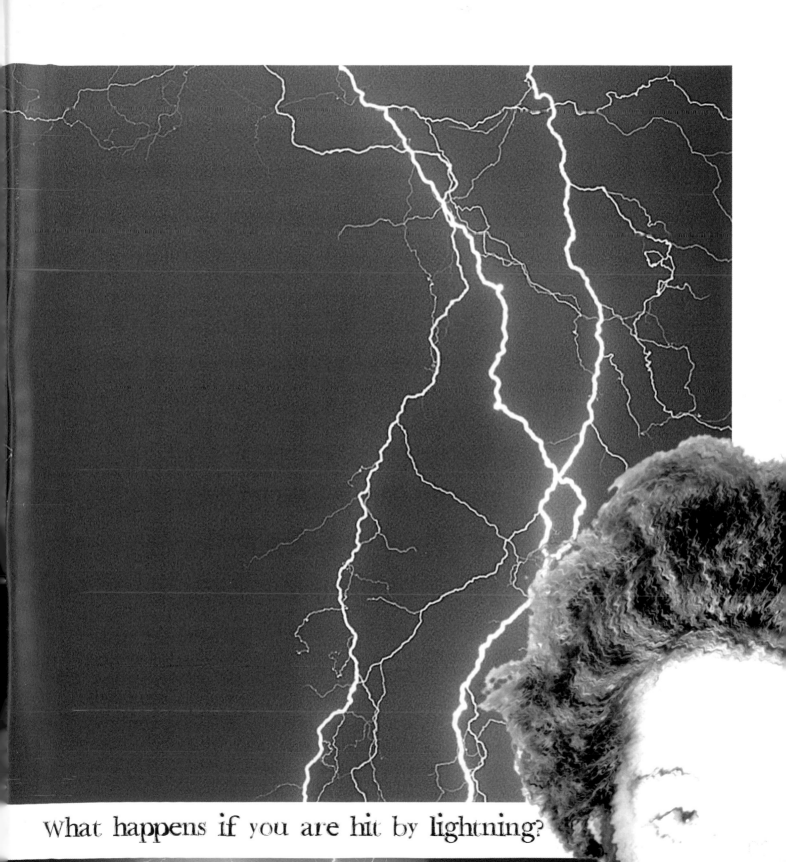

What happens if you are hit by lightning?